OVER-THE-COUNTER DRUGS

OVER-THE-COUNTER
DRUGS
BY ANN E. WEISS

A GROLIER COMPANY

FRANKLIN WATTS
NEW YORK I LONDON
TORONTO I SYDNEY I 1984
AN IMPACT BOOK

Photographs courtesy of
United Press International: pp. 3, 4, 29;
New York Public Library Picture Collection: pp. 11, 14;
FDA *Consumer* : p. 22; Ginger Giles: p. 38;
Proprietary Association: p. 29;
Sam Falk from Monkmeyer Press Photo Service: p. 62.

Library of Congress Cataloging in Publication Data

Weiss, Ann E., 1943-
Over-the-counter drugs.

(An Impact book)
Bibliography: p.
Includes index.
Summary: Discusses the over-the-counter drug industry,
including the history of regulation, safety tests, the
role of advertising in sales, and the controversy of
future deregulation.
1. Nonprescription drug industry—United States—
Juvenile literature. [1. Nonprescription drug industry.
2. Drugs] I. Title.
HD9666.5.W44   1983   338.4'76151'0973   83-21693
ISBN 0-531-04760-1

CONTENTS

TO MALCOLM

OVER-THE-COUNTER DRUGS

1

POISON!

It was September 29, 1982, and Lieutenant Philip Cappitelli was at home, enjoying a busman's holiday. Lieutenant Cappitelli is a member of the fire department in Arlington Heights, Illinois, a suburb of Chicago. Although September 29 was officially his day off, he kept his radio tuned to the emergency band, monitoring local police and fire calls.

By late afternoon, Lieutenant Cappitelli was thoroughly puzzled. In midmorning, he had heard a routine call for paramedics to assist at an apparent heart attack case on South Mitchell Avenue. The sick man, a twenty-seven-year-old postal worker named Adam Janus, had been rushed to Northwest Community Hospital.

Then, in the middle of the afternoon, came another call for paramedics to go to South Mitchell Avenue. This time, Lieutenant Cappitelli's radio informed him, there seemed to be two more heart attack victims. They turned out to be Adam Janus's twenty-five-year-old brother, Stanley, and Stanley's wife, Theresa.

How likely was it, Cappitelli wondered, that three people would all have heart attacks in the same house on the same day? Not very, he decided. Could some fast-acting virus or bacteria be responsible for the illnesses instead?

At Northwest Community Hospital, doctors were asking themselves the same thing. If a microorganism was responsible, they knew, it was a deadly one. Adam Janus had died six hours after being admitted. Now his brother was dead, too. His sister-in-law was dying.

There had been a fourth mysterious illness that same day, Lieutenant Cappitelli soon learned. When his mother-in-law came home from work, she reported that the twelve-year-old daughter of one of her co-workers had died early that morning—apparently of a heart attack—in the nearby town of Elk Grove. An emergency crew, summoned by the girl's parents, had been unable to help her. For a healthy twelve-year-old to have a fatal heart atack is almost unheard of.

What could be going on? Lieutenant Cappitelli telephoned a friend and fellow fire fighter, Richard Keyworth. Keyworth, who lives in Elk Grove, also monitors police and fire calls in his spare time. Did Keyworth know any details about the emergency calls? Cappitelli asked.

Keyworth did not, so the two men decided to call their fire stations and get more information. Minutes later, they were comparing notes.

The girl who had died in Elk Grove, Keyworth told Cappitelli, had been a healthy child, but she had waked up that morning with a cold and a sore throat. Her parents had given her a Tylenol capsule. She died almost at once.

Oddly enough, Tylenol also figured in the story Cappitelli had gotten from his colleagues at the Arlington Heights fire station. Adam Janus had felt unwell that morning, and he, too, had taken a Tylenol capsule. After he died, grieving relatives gathered at his home. His brother Stanley complained of a headache and took a Tylenol. Theresa Janus decided to take one as well.

-2-

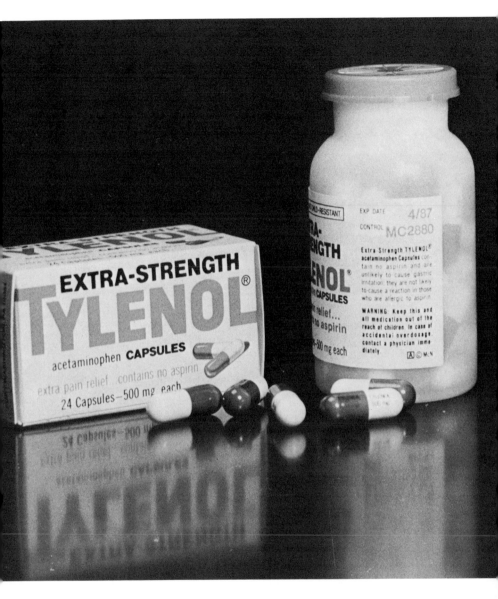

Seven people in the Chicago area died after taking Tylenol capsules such as these, which had been contaminated with cyanide.

*In the wake of the poisonings, Tylenol was
removed from the shelves of many stores, including
this Jewel Food Store on Chicago's Northside.*

Tylenol had to be the link among the four cases. Keyworth and Cappitelli notified their superiors of their suspicions. By next morning, the word was out in the suburbs of Chicago: Don't take Tylenol capsules. They may be deadly.

But for three other people, the warning did not come in time. The three, all young women, also died after taking Tylenol. By Friday, October 1, Tylenol capsules were known to have killed a total of seven people in the Chicago area. Autopsies showed that all seven deaths were due to cyanide, one of the most toxic—poisonous—substances known. Somehow, cyanide had gotten into Tylenol capsules in at least eight bottles sold in Illinois stores.

Now people panicked in earnest. Around Chicago, police and fire fighters visited schools and nursing homes, telling people to beware of Tylenol capsules. They passed out mimeographed warnings and tacked them to walls and doors. In some neighborhoods, police cars cruised the streets sounding the message over loudspeakers. Similarly equipped cars met commuter trains in various towns and villages.

Tylenol sales plummeted. The federal government in Washington, D.C., warned consumers not to buy or use any of the capsules. In some parts of the country, Tylenol was no longer even on the shelves. The state of Colorado completely banned sales of the capsules there. In Chicago, and in the states of North Dakota and Massachusetts, stores were not permitted to sell any Tylenol products—capsules, pills, or liquids.

The company that manufactures Tylenol, McNeil Consumer Products Company, lost no time in reacting to the emergency. Neither did Johnson & Johnson, the company that owns McNeil. First, Johnson & Johnson recalled—took back—ninety-three thousand bottles of Tylenol capsules from stores and individuals around the country. These bottles were marked by a number that showed they had been manufactured in the same batch as the capsules that caused the deaths in Elk Grove and Arlington Heights. When the three other deaths were reported, the company announced further recalls. In all, thirty-one million bottles of Tylenol capsules were returned to the manufacturer to be destroyed. Johnson & Johnson estimated that the recall cost the company $100 million.

Did the recall mean that McNeil or Johnson & Johnson was to blame for the cyanide being in the capsules? No. The poisoned capsules had been manufactured at a McNeil plant in Fort Washington, Pennsylvania. By September 30, inspectors from the Food and Drug Administration (FDA)—the federal government agency responsible for regulating drugs and medicines sold to the American public—had visited the Pennsylvania plant. They found no sign of cyanide contamination there. At the same time, federal, state, and local police agents investigating the Illinois deaths were finding clear proof that the capsules had been tampered with only after they had entered the state.

But if McNeil and Johnson & Johnson were not guilty of causing the seven deaths, who was? Someone with a grudge against one of the companies? With a grudge against one of the stores where the poisoned capsules were bought? Someone who hoped to use the poisoning to extort money from Johnson & Johnson? A person who wanted to murder just one of the seven victims and had not minded killing six other people in order to disguise his or her motive? Someone who was insane? No one knew the answer. As the weeks and months went by, and the Tylenol case remained unsolved, people began to accept the fact that they might never know.

To add to the confusion, similar cases popped up in other parts of the country throughout the fall of 1982. A man in California went to the hospital with strychnine poisoning after taking a Tylenol capsule. He recovered. Harmful or deadly substances were also found in other pain relievers, in eye drops, and in some foods. Suddenly, no one seemed safe. Serious illness—even death— could strike through the most innocent-seeming product.

Fear made people cautious. As Tylenol sales slipped, so did sales of other pain relievers and sleep aids that are sold "over the counter," without a doctor's prescription. In the week that followed the Illinois deaths, one drug store chain reported a 16.5 percent drop in sales of over-the-counter (OTC) items. Near Chicago, sales were off by nearly 40 percent.

But the wave of fear had its positive aspects. People began considering how they might protect themselves and others against deadly tampering with drugs and other products in the future. One obvious solution seemed to be tamper-resistant packaging. Even before the Tylenol scare, some drugs were being packaged with seals or other devices that would alert the buyer if the container had already been opened. Now, consumer advocates began demanding that the FDA require all OTC drugs to be marketed in tamper-resistant packages.

Others were thinking beyond packaging to OTC drugs themselves. McNeil and Johnson & Johnson were not responsible for the contamination of their product, and during the crisis, the companies had dealt forthrightly with the public and with the FDA. But are all companies equally forthright all the time? people asked. Do they always put the consumer first and company profits second?

There were other questions. Are all OTC drugs safe? Effective? Necessary? Or are Americans, prompted by slick ads in newspapers and magazines, on radio and television, spending billions of dollars a year on products of little or no medical value?

2

FROM HOLLYHOCK TO MODERN DRUGS

The story of mankind's use of drugs and medicines goes back many thousands of years. It may have started with hollyhocks.

Pollen from hollyhock flowers has been found in the Shanidar Cave in Iraq's Zagros Mountains. Sixty thousand years ago, Shanidar was a burial place for a group of the Stone Age people we call Neanderthals. From the position of the pollen, it is clear that hollyhocks were carefully placed in one of the Neanderthal graves there. Bits of pollen remains from seven other kinds of flowers were found beside the same skeleton.

Most of the flowers belonged to plants that are believed to have some medicinal value. In Iraq today, people still use hollyhock roots, leaves, seeds, and flowers to treat toothaches, inflammations, and open wounds. Of the seven other kinds of plants buried in the grave at Shanidar sixty thousand years ago, six are listed by the modern Iraqi Ministry of Agriculture as medically useful.

Plants and their flowers have been a source of medicine around the world. Five thousand years ago, the Chinese drew up a list of plants they used for healing. One of them was an herb, *ma huang*. Today, we use *ma huang*—which we call ephedrine—in nose drops and inhalers.

The ancient Egyptians also relied on plants to treat illness. Archaeologists working in Egypt have discovered a thirty-five-hundred-year-old list of eight hundred healing plants. Among them is colchicum, which is derived from the seeds and roots of the autumn crocus. In large amounts, colchicum is a deadly poison. In tiny doses, it is highly effective against the painful inflammation of gout.

Later civilizations also used plants as medicines. The Indians of North and South America did, and so did the ancient Greeks and Romans. In A.D. 754, the world's first known apothecary shop was opened by an Arab in the city of Baghdad. Even in the Dark Ages that followed the collapse of the old Roman Empire in Europe, doctors and herbalists carried on their craft.

Back then, medicine and pharmacy were a single science. Healers diagnosed illness, prepared their own drugs, and treated patients with them. In 1240, though, that changed in Europe. The Holy Roman Emperor Frederick II ordered a separation between the practice of medicine and the preparation of drugs. The new decree led, over the years, to the establishment of many apothecary shops. One of them, founded in 1688 by the German pharmacist Friedrich Jacob Merck, was the direct forerunner of the modern American drug firm of Merck, Sharp, and Dohme.

By the seventeenth century, pharmacy had become a business. In England, many of those who invented new drugs took care to patent their inventions so that no one else could copy them. Taking out a patent required the inventor to list all of a drug's ingredients, either on its label or marked on the glass of the medicine bottle itself. However, those who wished to keep their formulas secret could do so simply by failing to apply for a patent.

*This twelfth-century drawing shows
herbs being dug up from the ground
and made into medicines.*

Medicines, both patented and unpatented, quickly found their way across the Atlantic Ocean and into the new American colonies. Both kinds of drugs were available in apothecary shops and both were heavily advertised in newspapers. Because of this, patented drugs and unpatented ones became confused in people's minds. Before long, all drugs were being referred to as "patent" whether or not they really were.

What were "patent" medicines like? Robert Turlington's Balsam of Life, patented in England during the eighteenth century, listed twenty-six ingredients. All twenty-six were derived from plants—some imported from the Orient, others picked in English fields.

Balsam of Life purported to cure a wide variety of ailments. So did Chinese Stones, recommended by their inventor for treatment of toothache, cancer, rabies, and snakebite. A more specific remedy was Hooper's Female Pills, sold exclusively to women. More specific still was the balm offered for sale by the mother-in-law of the American printer and statesman Benjamin Franklin. She called it "her well-known Ointment for the ITCH."

After the American Revolution, the new United States Congress established its own patent law. The first medicine patented under it was a preparation called Samuel Lea's Bilious Pills. They were compounded of gamboge, aloes, nitrate of potash, and soap. People bought the pills as a cure for bilious and yellow fevers, jaundice, dysentery, dropsy, worms, and "female complaints."

The patent medicine business flourished in the United States. In 1804, a New York company listed just ninety available drugs. A century later, in 1906, a committee of Congress listed more than fifty thousand.

Over fifty thousand drugs—and most of them useless, the committee found. A large percentage of them were downright dangerous. For example, there were the medicines made up of a few plant ingredients in an alcohol base. One such medicine was Lydia Pinkham's Vegetable Compound. Lydia Pinkham's contained 18 percent alcohol. Women who relied on it to give them that glowing sense of well-being never suspected that they might be on their way to a lifetime of alcoholism. Another popular remedy, Cuforhedake Brane-Fude, was 34 percent alcohol. Even worse were children's cough syrups made with derivatives of opium. Parents found these medicines a wonderful help—they invariably sent restless young ones into a deep sleep. They were also turning infants and toddlers into drug addicts.

Other preparations were more innocuous. A man named William Radam made a fortune selling his Microbe Killer. The fact that tiny organisms called microbes cause certain diseases was only discovered in the first years of the twentieth century, and Radam capitalized on that new knowledge to market his product. It would, he maintained, kill every kind of microbe, and thus, cure all disease. When United States government scientists analyzed Radam's Microbe Killer, they found it consisted of 99.381 percent water and less than half of one percent hydrochloric and sulphuric acids. In addition, the scientists discovered, Radam put in a few drops of red wine for coloring.

Many members of Congress were disturbed by the fact that Americans were wasting their money on "medicines" like the Microbe Killer—and destroying their health with preparations laced with narcotics and alcohol. So, on June 30, 1906, they passed the Pure Food and Drug Act.

The new law allowed the federal government to act against products that it could prove were harmful or falsely labeled. The government could ask a judge to order such products seized, and the manufacturer could be fined or imprisoned. Enforcement of the law was in the hands of the Bureau of Chemistry, a division of the United States Department of Agriculture. Later, in 1931,

a new agency, the Food and Drug Administration, was created. Today, the FDA is responsible for enforcing pure food and drug laws. It is part of the Department of Health and Human Services.

It soon became apparent that the 1906 law was not going to be enough to keep useless and dangerous drugs off the market. It did nothing to prevent people from producing and advertising any kind of drug they wanted to, no matter how useless or dangerous it might be. All that the law required was accurate labeling. As one federal judge commented in 1922, "No law prohibits a man from making any medicine he wants to and selling it to the people if he tells the truth about it."

The judge was right. Worthless, harmful drugs continued to flood the market. People—who generally did not read, or did not understand, the labels—continued to buy them. A stricter law was needed.

It was to be years before the country had such a law. Not until 1933 was a new pure food and drug bill introduced in Congress. Even then, Congress continued to delay. Months and years went by, and the bill failed to be enacted into law. Then, tragedy struck.

The tragedy involved Elixir Sulfanilamide, which was manufactured at a small plant in Tennessee. In September 1938, 240 gallons (710 liters) of it were distributed around the country. The Elixir had been carefully tested at the plant for appearance, fragrance, and flavor—but not for safety. Within a month, one hundred or more people in fifteen states had died after taking it.

At the turn of the century
thousands of patent medicines
made extraordinary claims
for their healing powers.

Cause of death: poisoning by diethylene glycol, one of the Elixir's ingredients.

At once, the FDA seized stocks of the pink liquid and took them off the market. Only by a lucky fluke was the FDA able to act so promptly. The preparation was mislabeled. Technically, an elixir had to contain alcohol, and Elixir Sulfanilamide did not. Had it not been for the error, the FDA would have been legally powerless to protect the public from the deadly drug.

That was the prod Congress needed. Lawmakers at last began work on the five-year-old food and drug bill. They passed it, and President Franklin D. Roosevelt signed it into law before the year's end.

The Food, Drug, and Cosmetics Act of 1938 required drug manufacturers to test new products for safety *before* offering them for sale. What's more, the findings of those safety tests had to be reported to the FDA. A company that did not test a product, or that failed to report the results of those tests fully and honestly, might find that product seized by the FDA.

Thirteen years later, the 1938 act was amended. In 1951, Congress passed a bill that separated drugs into two groups, prescription and nonprescription, or over-the-counter. Before that, there had been no such distinction.

Prescription drugs were to be those that the FDA considered so new, or so powerful, or so habit-forming, that they were better given only by order of a doctor and under a doctor's care. Penicillin and other antibiotics, medicines for the treatment of heart disease and high blood pressure, and powerful tranquilizers were among the drugs classed as prescription-only.

OTC drugs, on the other hand, were preparations considered harmless enough for people to prescribe for themselves. Cold remedies such as chest rubs, gargles, and throat lozenges are examples. So are many diet aids, pain relievers like aspirin, some sleeping pills, and many more. It is estimated that there were over three hundred thousand different OTC drugs available to Americans in 1982.

Sometimes a drug can move from one group to the other. Usually the movement is out of the prescription-only class and into the nonprescription class. That is because scientists know that a new drug may seem safe at first, and only turn out to have harmful side effects over the long term. So the FDA may order that a drug start out as a prescription item and then, after years of a good safety record, move it to the nonprescription class. As we will see later, Tylenol is one drug that made the switch from prescription to nonprescription.

The 1938 Food, Drug, and Cosmetics Act was stronger than the 1906 measure. But even after 1951, serious flaws remained. The most important one was that the law did not force drug makers to demonstrate that their products were effective, as well as safe. In other words, although Elixir Sulfanilamide could not have been sold legally after 1938, a preparation like Radam's Microbe Killer might have been.

Congress did not attempt to close this loophole until 1962, although bills that would have dealt with it earlier were offered well before that. Again, it took a tragedy to get Congress going. This time the tragedy concerned a drug called thalidomide.

Thalidomide, a sleeping pill, first went on sale in West Germany in the late 1950s. It seemed to be a real wonder drug. It produced deep, restful sleep, with no apparent side effects, such as a morning-after "hung over" feeling. It was particularly effective with pregnant women. By 1960, thalidomide was being used in England, Canada, Portugal, Australia, and South America. In some places, it was being sold over the counter. Its American manufacturer, the William S. Merrell Company, was urging the FDA to approve it for sale in this country, too.

Then scientists began noticing mysterious increases in birth defects in countries where thalidomide was in use. Children whose mothers had taken the drug in the months before their births were born armless or legless, or both. Today, over five thousand "thalidomide babies" are reaching adulthood in Europe.

The thalidomide story came to light early in 1962, but not until midsummer did the American public become alarmed by it. At the same time, the public learned that it was only thanks to the FDA—and especially to one FDA doctor, Frances O. Kelsey—that the Merrell Company had never been able to offer thalidomide for sale in the United States.

That brought home to Americans the importance of the FDA and led to an outcry in favor of strengthening the agency. At last, Congress got down to work, and in October 1962, President John F. Kennedy signed new legislation into law.

This legislation gave the FDA wider powers than ever before. It required drug makers to test their products for effectiveness as well as for safety. For the first time, the FDA was in a position to see to it that the drugs we use are both safe and effective.

3

TESTING DRUGS

To see that drugs sold in this country are safe and effective, the FDA has set up rules and procedures for drug companies to follow in developing and testing new products. The rules and procedures are complex and long, and they apply only to ingredients that are new since 1938.

Most OTC medicines are compounded of drugs known since before that date. That means most OTC items are exempt from FDA new-drug rules. However, a prescription drug developed since 1938 can become a nonprescription drug, and in that case, it will have gone through the official testing procedure. As we will see in chapter six, hundreds of current prescription-only drugs may be made available over the counter within a few years. Also, as we will see, government agencies may require certain tests on nonprescription drugs in specific circumstances. For example, a drug company may have to prove that its product lives up to a particular advertising claim. When that happens, some, although not all, of the new-drug testing procedures will be applied to the OTC item.

What are those procedures? Suppose chemists at a drug manufacturing firm come up with a compound they think will be medically useful. They call it compound Y.

We'll start by assuming that executives at the drug company are interested in compound Y. They think it is a good type of drug for their company to market, and they believe that people will buy it. So they begin the process of getting the FDA to approve its sale.

The first step is to order a thorough analysis—chemical, biological, and pharmaceutical—of the compound. The analysts' job is to determine exactly what substances are in the drug and whether any of them might be toxic. They also look to see if anything in it might be likely to produce unexpected side effects, such as raising or lowering patients' blood pressure, or making them more susceptible to infection.

If the results of this screening are satisfactory, compound Y moves on to the next stage: a toxicity study. Toxicity studies are generally carried out on animals—mice, rats, and dogs. In some cases, other animals, such as hamsters, guinea pigs, rabbits, or monkeys, are also used.

The first step in a toxicity study may be an LD_{50} test. LD_{50} stands for "lethal dose fifty." It is the dose of a drug strong enough to kill 50 percent of the animals used in the test. Although the LD_{50} test is traditional in American and European drug testing, it is not actually required by the FDA. Today many scientists, here and in other countries, argue that it is not even necessary. A drug's toxicity, they contend, can be determined by the other, more sophisticated, animal tests that follow. Many drugs currently awaiting FDA approval have not been subjected to an LD_{50} test.

With or without an LD_{50}, compound Y goes on to other animal tests. These "preclinical" studies examine the effects of dosages of differing sizes. They help company scientists decide what the ideal human dose will be. They also allow researchers to predict the effects of an overdose, and permit them to work out possible treatments for such an overdose.

The amount of time devoted to preclinical animal studies varies, depending on what kind of drug compound Y is. If it is intended to be used for a short time, in order to treat an acute illness such as a cold or the flu, the animals will be given the drug for only a few days. If it is for the treatment of a chronic long-term condition such as high blood pressure or diabetes, the tests may last for two or three months. Throughout, the animals' health is carefully monitored. Their urine and blood are checked regularly. At the end of the tests, the animals are killed— "sacrificed." Their internal organs are examined to see what effects, if any, the drug has had on them.

More laboratory tests follow. These are long-range toxicity studies. Rats, dogs, and other animals may be given doses of compound Y for a year or more. Again, the animals are watched for any sign of harmful or unexpected side effects. Special tests may be designed to show the drug's effect on pregnant animals or to see whether or not it causes birth defects.

Only now is compound Y brought to the attention of the FDA. The drug company prepares a Notice of Claimed *I*nvestigational Exemption for a *N*ew *D*rug— known as an IND—and sends it to the agency. According to FDA rules, the IND must set forth everything the company knows or suspects about the drug and its possible toxic effects, as well as complete background information about the scientists, doctors, and other researchers who carried out the early studies on it.

If the FDA finds the IND satisfactory, it will give its approval for the next stage in the development of a new drug—its clinical testing in human beings.

Up to this point, the work on compound Y has been mostly concerned with toxicity. From now on, in the human studies, the emphasis will be on effectiveness as well. Generally, these studies fall into three categories.

First are the pharmacological studies. These are usually carried out on healthy volunteers and are

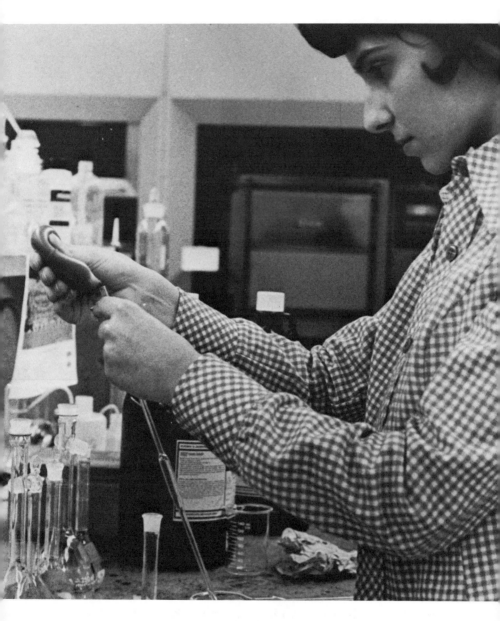

This woman is studying chemical compounds in a FDA laboratory.

designed to indicate the best ways to use compound Y in order for patients to get the most benefit from it. The researchers are looking for answers to specific questions. What is the best dosage of compound Y under various circumstances? Should a patient take one large dose a day or four smaller ones? Does this drug work better if it is taken before meals or after them? Is it more effective in people of a particular age?

The second category of tests consists of trials in patients who have the illness or condition that compound Y is intended to treat. These tests will show how effective the drug is in individual cases. Finally, there will be tests on large numbers of actual patients. These studies are most useful for predicting how well compound Y will work over the long run.

Researchers need to take great pains to make sure their clinical tests are accurate. For instance, suppose compound Y is a medication for the common cold. Clinical tests show that people with colds who use the drug get better. But would they have improved anyway, without using compound Y? After all, colds do eventually go away on their own, even without medication. To make sure their results are dependable, scientists can rely on two devices—placebos and double-blind tests.

A placebo is a preparation that a patient believes is effective, but which is really inert—inactive—as a drug. In this case, the placebo will look, smell, feel, and taste as much as possible like compound Y. In reality, however, it will be a harmless but useless preparation—a sugar pill, perhaps, or flavored, colored water. In the clinical test, researchers will divide the test patients into two groups. Half will be given compound Y and half will get the placebo. Then the researchers will watch to see how quickly the people in each group get over their colds.

Strange as it may seem, some of those who get the placebo may get well as rapidly as those taking the medicine. Why? Because they will believe they are getting a powerful new drug. That belief alone may be enough to make them feel better—even to be better!

But on balance, for compound Y to be considered effective, the people taking it should recover from their colds faster than those getting the placebo. If they do not, that will be clinical proof that compound Y is no more effective than a sugar pill or than tinted water.

Placebos are also used in double-blind tests. In such tests, however, neither the patients nor the researchers know which group is getting the medicine and which is getting the placebo.

There is a good reason for that. If a doctor is confident that he or she is giving a patient an effective medicine, the patient may sense that confidence. If, on the other hand, the doctor knows that the "medicine" is a useless placebo, he or she may offer it casually, even reluctantly. The patient may sense that reluctance. Such a negative feeling may delay recovery, just as a positive one may speed it up. So a double-blind experiment, in which neither patient nor researcher knows who is getting compound Y and who is not (until the experiment is over), is the most reliable way to test a drug clinically.

Once the clinical tests are complete, the drug company turns to the FDA once more. It files a New Drug Application (NDA).

An NDA contains reports of all the tests that have been carried out from the beginning. It is a fuller, more detailed report than an IND. In addition to explaining the drug's test performance, it includes information about how it will be packaged, labeled, and sold.

The FDA has six months to respond to the NDA, although it may work out an agreement with the company to take more time if necessary. The FDA has a choice of responses.

- It can approve compound Y and give the manufacturer the go-ahead to begin selling it.

- It can refuse to approve.
- It can demand more testing.
- It can ask for more information or for more evidence of the drug's safety and effectiveness.
- It can ask for different packaging or for clearer labeling.

In the case of a drug that is effective yet which may produce undesirable side effects, the FDA might order inclusion of a special warning in each package.

Getting FDA approval for a new drug takes time—years in some cases. Surely, a process so long and elaborate ought to guarantee that all the medicines available to us in this country are both safe and effective. Unfortunately, it does not.

Item: In the fall of 1982, three nonprescription drugs, Sober Up!, Sober Aid, and Sober Up Time, went on the market. Billed as "booze blockers" by their manufacturers, these products were supposed to cancel out the effects of drinking alcohol. Go out to a bar or to a party, get drunk, swallow a dose, and drive home completely safe and sober—that was the sales pitch.

Item: For decades, phenacetin, a drug found in various OTC painkillers, as well as in some prescription medicines, had been suspected of causing blood disorders and cancer. Recent studies have demonstrated the link. Besides that, according to the FDA, "prolonged excessive ingestion of any common analgesic [painkilling] product containing phenacetin will significantly increase the probability of serious kidney disease and premature death." Put more simply, that meant that people who used a lot of phenacetin-containing drugs stood a better-than-average chance of dying early of kidney failure. Yet the drug remained on the market until mid-1983.

Item: Recent studies suggest that giving aspirin to children when they are sick with a virus can lead to their death from a rare disease known as Reye's Syndrome. Reye's syndrome is characterized by vomiting, lethargy, and confusion or irritability. Eventually, the victim falls into a coma. Death often follows. An investigation by a team of researchers in Ohio showed that of ninety-seven children with Reye's, ninety-four had been given aspirin just before developing the disease.

Children dying from aspirin? OTC painkillers that may cause serious illness and death? "Remedies" that seem guaranteed to put thousands of drunk drivers on the road? How is this possible, given the FDA's apparently stringent testing and approval requirements for drugs?

There are many answers. One involves the fact that most OTC drugs, such as aspirin, for example, were developed before 1938. They are not covered by FDA new-drug testing rules.

Does that mean that unscrupulous people can ignore those rules—and market unsafe or useless drugs? Sometimes that happens, as we will see. But in general, the situation is more complicated. Even a thoroughly-tested drug—for instance, a prescription-only item later sold over the counter—may prove to be unreliable or dangerous. When that happens, it is likely to be the result of problems inherent in any animal or clinical testing program.

To begin with, it is not always easy to translate the results of tests on animals into human terms. Animals are not people. Their bodies are different. Animals are not susceptible to many of the illnesses and health conditions that plague us humans. Some of their medical and physical responses differ markedly from those of human beings.

Such differences make it harder for scientists to take the results of animal tests and predict the implications of those tests for people. True, animal tests can be a means of flushing out dangerously toxic substances—that is one justification for the LD_{50} test. But other test results may be less cut-and-dried. For instance, if one milligram of a substance causes an adverse reaction in a one-pound (.45-kg) test animal, is that substance nevertheless safe for a 120-pound (55-kg) human?

Scientists have come up with some ingenious ways to try to answer such questions. Suppose they are testing a drug intended for the treatment of high blood pressure—hypertension. Early tests show that the drug does lower blood pressure in laboratory animals. But what if a person taking it undergoes unusual amounts of stress? What if he or she combines it with large amounts of alcohol, or with other medications? How will it work then?

To find out in animal tests, researchers can subject the creatures they are working with to approximations of the conditions under which humans might use the drug. They might reproduce external stress with flashing lights or noisy buzzers, or some other system designed to upset and distress the animals. They might feed the animals alcohol or other substances and observe their reactions.

Such experiments do work—to an extent. But by themselves, animal tests are far from satisfactory. That is why the drug must go on to studies in human patients.

But clinical studies have their own drawbacks. They are another reason unsafe and ineffective drugs find their way onto the market.

In the first place, clinical studies may not last long enough. Some drugs have serious side effects that take years to show up. Phenacetin is such a drug.

So should the FDA require drug companies to test each new drug for a much longer time, ten or twenty years perhaps? Drug company executives respond that that would be impractical. It would cost too much. Besides, it would mean keeping many good and useful drugs off the market for too long. Some drugs don't require a ten-year testing period. For others, ten years might not be enough. But it's impossible to tell ahead of time just which drugs are which. Requiring a decade or more of clinical trials for all new drugs would deprive thousands of patients of medicines that they might otherwise be benefiting from.

In the second place, some clinical testing is impossible to do. It would not be ethical.

Take aspirin. Giving it to children when they have a virus may cause some of them to develop Reye's Syndrome. But no one is going to design an experiment to find out for sure if there is a link between aspirin and Reye's. No parent would allow a child to take part in an experiment that might well prove fatal. No doctor would run it. No hospital would sponsor it. No state would allow it.

The same is true of tests on pregnant women. Doctors suspect that some drugs, including aspirin, may be responsible for certain birth defects. But no one is going to experiment on mothers-to-be—and risk killing or injuring unborn children—in order to find out.

Another drawback to clinical testing is that it cannot be done on a scale large enough to uncover every problem that might occur in actual medical practice. The Zomax case proves that.

In the spring of 1983, Johnson & Johnson announced it was taking Zomax, one of its prescription pain relievers, off the market, at least temporarily. Zomax, the company acknowledged, had been responsible for at least five deaths and many more cases of illness.

But these were five deaths out of fifteen million Zomax users. Before the FDA approved the drug, it had been clinically tested in only about three thousand subjects—far too small a number to reveal that Zomax can produce an allergic reaction in a tiny percentage of the population. Unless Johnson & Johnson executives had ordered Zomax tested in millions upon millions of people, they could not have known its dangers. And such

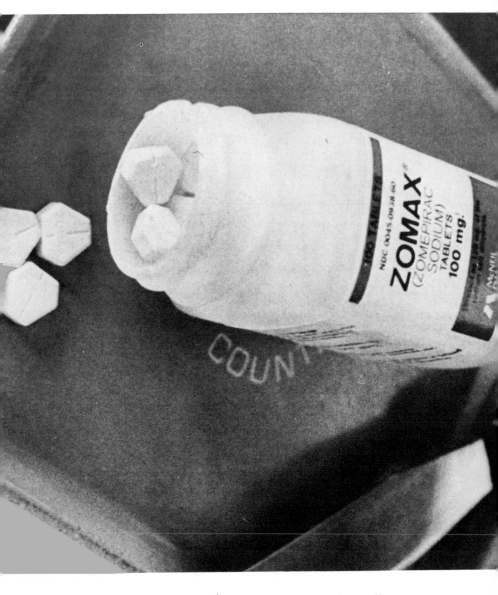

The prescription drug Zomax was taken off the market in 1983 when it was found to have caused illness, and even death, in some people.

large-scale testing is clearly impossible. As far as anyone could tell, Zomax testing was adequate under FDA rules.

For some other drugs, however, testing is not adequate. In some cases, the doctors running a test may neglect to set up complex double-blind experiments. In others, they may fail to check the performance of a new drug against a useless placebo. Either can produce unreliable results.

Inadequate testing can also relate to the way the people who carry out the tests are reimbursed for their efforts. Drug companies pay doctors for conducting clinical tests on their products. Can getting a fee from a company lead a doctor, consciously or unconsciously, to produce the very results that the company wants? It has happened.

Sometimes, sloppy testing procedures give way to something that borders on outright fraud. Sober Up!, for example, was "tested" by a high school social studies teacher and a dentist who was a personal friend of the president of the company that manufactured the product. The testing and analysis of Sober Aid and Sober Up Time were somewhat more careful, but in each case, experts say, the manufacturer seems to have exaggerated the study's positive findings and ignored its negative ones.

The FDA summed up its opinion of the testing in this way: "The FDA is unaware of adequate and well-controlled scientific studies which demonstrate that any product or ingredient can prevent or minimize inebriation." Within days, all three products were off the market.

The case of the booze blockers is an extreme example, and none of the companies involved was a major American drug firm. But even large, highly respected drug companies have been known to be involved in the inadequate or deceptive testing of drugs.

Over the years, the federal government has had to order several companies, including Warner-Lambert, Johnson & Johnson, and Lever Brothers, to stop selling their OTC mouthwashes as "germ killing" cold cures. A report prepared by the National Academy of Sciences maintained that for killing germs, rinsing the mouth with plain water was as effective as using one of these products. At about the same time, a bronchial inhaler manufactured by Merck, Sharp, and Dohme was shown to be ineffective against asthma, bronchitis, and emphysema. If any of the four companies had test results that backed up their claims, they must have used very inexacting testing procedures indeed.

People who bought mouthwashes thinking they would cure a cold, or inhalers believing they would take care of an asthma attack, were being cheated. Being cheated is not good, but it's not the worst thing that can happen to a consumer. Sometimes, drug company deception regarding test results can be life-threatening.

An oral contraceptive put on the market by Eli Lilly and Company, for instance, was shown to induce breast tumors in test animals. Test results of a similar contraceptive, manufactured by the Upjohn Company, also indicated a link with the disease. Yet even with the evidence before them, executives at both companies were reluctant to act. Only after large amounts of publicity—largely unfavorable—were the drugs withdrawn.

Lilly was involved in a more recent scandal. In April 1982, the company won FDA approval for Oraflex, a prescription drug for arthritis sufferers. In August, the FDA hastily reversed that approval, and banned the drug. During the four months in between, fifty Americans had died after using Oraflex.

That was bad enough. Worse, the FDA found that people at Lilly knew, while the FDA was considering its approval, that, under the name Opren, the drug had already caused twenty-six deaths in England. In addition, the FDA said, Lilly neglected to report "promptly" a total of ninety-six Opren-Oraflex-related deaths, sixty-two of which occurred before the drug was approved.

Of course, Oraflex, like the oral contraceptives, was a prescription drug, not an OTC item. But after all, prescription drugs can make the switch to nonprescription status. Right now, the FDA is considering making hundreds of potent prescription items available over the counter. The possibility of potentially hazardous OTC drugs making it to the shelves of your local drugstore or supermarket is a very real one.

Drug company executives are quick to defend themselves and their companies against charges that their drug testing procedures are either dishonest or inadequate. Any problems, they say, are merely the problems inherent in any laboratory or clincial testing program. Some of these problems—the limits of drawing conclusions from animal tests, the relatively small numbers involved in clinical testing, ethical considerations, and the difficulty of designing studies that cover all the ways a drug may be used—are inevitable, they maintain.

The executives remind their critics that they spend a great deal of time and money each year on researching new drugs and trying them out. Many of the advances of modern medical science have come from drug company labs. It is partly thanks to these companies that Americans enjoy general good health and such a long life expectancy today.

But having spent huge sums of money to develop and test a drug, company executives agree, they are naturally eager to begin earning back that money by getting the drug on the market as soon as possible. After all, their firms are in business to make a profit. And it is in the hope of making a profit that company officials go on to the next step in the making and marketing of a product. That step is advertising.

4

ADVERTISING DRUGS

Over-the-counter drugs are a big business. In 1981, Americans used $70 million worth of Alka-Seltzer. They spent $85 million on Bayer aspirin, $95 million on Bufferin, and $365 million on Tylenol. A total of $486 million went for over-the-counter cough syrups, drops, and lozenges. In all, in 1981, Americans spent $6 billion on nonprescription drugs.

Six billion dollars is a lot of money, but three hundred thousand OTC drugs are all competing for a share of it. So making a profit requires offering a product that people are eager to buy. Making them eager to buy requires advertising.

Sometimes the advertising comes first, even before the product.

In a book about the FDA, *200,000,000 Guinea Pigs,* writer John G. Fuller tells about Dr. William Beaver, a pharmacology professor at George Washington University, in Washington, D.C. Dr. Beaver was asked by an advertising agency to advise it about a new OTC pain reliever for which the agency was planning an ad campaign. Dr. Beaver was agreeable.

He was agreeable, that is, until he discovered that

the pain reliever did not yet exist. Rather than help the advertisers understand how a useful new drug worked so they could convey that information to the public, Dr. Beaver was supposed to help them figure out what sort of new drug the American public could be persuaded to buy. Then, and only then, would the drug company try to develop a product to fit.

Dr. Beaver did not care for this cynical approach to medicine, and he turned down the job. Almost certainly, though, the ad agency found someone else to take it. The product that resulted may be sitting in your medicine cabinet right now.

The kind of work Dr. Beaver was being asked to do is called market research. It is a vital element in the development of many OTC drugs.

Market research has several elements. First might come a look at the buying habits of Americans. What kinds of drugs are most popular? What size bottles or containers sell most rapidly? How does packaging affect sales? Market researchers study the answers to questions like these, and analyze them in detail as they plan for new products.

Next may come surveys and personal interviews. Researchers will question a cross-section of the population about the OTC drugs they already buy and use. They will ask what new kinds of products people would like to see available. What diseases or conditions should they be designed to treat? Should a new product be in the form of a pill, a liquid, a capsule, an ointment? What color should it be? What flavor? How much would people be willing to pay for it?

Finally, researchers try out possible advertising campaigns to see which one consumers seem to respond to most favorably. Such testing helps to answer questions such as the following: Should ads emphasize a product's speed or its potency? Which do consumers prefer, newness or old-fashioned reliability? What advertising slogans seem most persuasive? When the research is complete, drug company executives may have everything they need for selling the product—except, perhaps, the product itself.

However, putting the product together may not require a great deal of time or effort. Much of the "research" done to develop "new" OTC items merely consists of combining several old, familiar ingredients in a slightly different way. For example, a small amount of caffeine, which is a stimulant, may be added to an aspirin preparation. This "new" product can be advertised as a pain reliever that "peps you up." (Although it probably won't do the job as well as a single cup of coffee would.) Or aspirin might be combined with an antihistamine. Antihistamines produce sleepiness in many people. Result: a "new" kind of aspirin to take at bedtime.

Some aspirin products contain both caffeine and an antihistamine. The two additives may cancel each other out, but they do allow a drug company to advertise something that's "new" and "different." Just how new? Drug companies generally refuse to submit such combination drugs for FDA review, arguing that the products are not really new at all!

Of course, not all OTC drugs are developed this way. Some are the result of careful work designed to meet real medical needs. Tylenol is an example.

The story of Tylenol begins with the story of another OTC drug, aspirin. Aspirin is one of those substances that traces its roots far back into prehistory. Its essential ingredient is salicylic acid.

Salicylic acid is found in the bark of willow trees and in some other plants. Many ancient peoples, including the Indians of North America, brewed a kind of willow bark tea and used it to reduce fevers and to relieve aches and pain. When the sixteenth century French explorer Jacques Cartier and his men fell ill in the snowy woods of the New World, Indians gave them willow tea to drink.

The Frenchmen were astonished at how rapidly it made them feel better.

Not until the nineteenth century, though, did doctors in Europe and the United States begin to recognize the soothing effects of salicylic acid. Even then, they found it almost impossible to use as a medicine. Concentrated salicylic acid burned patients' throats and upset their stomachs. Finally, in 1893, a chemist at the German firm of Bayer and Company treated salicylic acid with acetic acid to produce acetylsalicylic acid.

Acetylsalicylic acid has the pain-relieving qualities of salicylic acid, but with fewer of its unpleasant side effects. By 1899, Bayer was selling acetylsalicylic acid under the name of aspirin.

Aspirin does not cure any illness or condition, but it treats the symptoms of many. It can be taken for a minor headache or to lower a fever, for a sore throat, to reduce the inflammation of arthritis, or as a postoperative analgesic. Aspirin has been described as the world's only true wonder drug.

Yet as aspirin gained in popularity, doctors began to learn that it, too, could produce side effects in some people. Patients reported that aspirin caused upset stomachs, ringing in the ears, slight deafness, or outbreaks of hives. In a few cases, taking aspirin interfered with the normal clotting of blood. In rare instances, people who took the drug died. For them, and for some with lesser allergies, a "nonaspirin aspirin" was needed.

In 1955, Johnson & Johnson put such a medicine on the market. It was Tylenol, whose principal ingredient is acetaminophen. Acetaminophen relieves pain and reduces fever, just as acetylsalicylic acid does. It seems to have no undesirable side effects. Acetaminophen's major drawback appears to be that it is not effective for arthritis patients, since, unlike aspirin, it does not reduce inflammation.

When it was introduced, Tylenol was a prescription-only drug, so advertising for it was directed exclusively at doctors and others in the medical profession. Tylenol ads appeared in medical newsletters and journals. Sales people for Johnson & Johnson promoted the new product vigorously. They visited pharmacists around the country, encouraging them to stock the drug. They urged doctors to order it for their patients.

The Tylenol ad campaign was effective. Within five years, doctors had prescribed the drug for millions of people with overwhelmingly positive results. In 1960, the FDA, impressed by Tylenol's record of safety and usefulness, reclassified it as a nonprescription item. Now, Johnson & Johnson was free to advertise it to the general public for OTC sales.

In 1975, that advertising began. Tylenol's ads suggested that doctors preferred Tylenol to aspirin. Sales boomed. By 1978, the drug was outselling all its nonaspirin competitors. It was also outselling what had once been the world's leading nonprescription pain reliever—Bayer aspirin.

In the United States, Bayer is manufactured and sold by Sterling Drug. Alarmed by Tylenol's inroads into its market, Sterling began promoting a nonaspirin Bayer. This promotion failed, and nonaspirin Bayer was withdrawn.

Next, Sterling executives decided to take on Tylenol's claim of doctor recommendation. "Makers of Tylenol, shame on you!" scolded Bayer commercials. Doctors do not recommend products by brand name, the Bayer ads went on. They just say, "Take an aspirin." Bayer, the ads concluded, is aspirin, and Tylenol is not. So doctors were really saying "Take a Bayer," not "Take a Tylenol."

Carrying through on their proaspirin line, Bayer ads went a step further. They began hinting that acetamino-

*Advertisements for OTC drugs
seek to capture consumers'
attention in a crowded market.*

phen might not be safe. "Leading experts have expressed great concern" about the drug, the ads contended.

What's interesting about this is that even as Sterling's Bayer ads were raising the specter of "great concern" about acetaminophen in Tylenol, Sterling was selling a pain reliever called Panadol. Panadol is 100 percent acetaminophen.

Before 1983, Panadol was marketed outside the United States. Now, it is appearing in American stores. The fears raised by the Tylenol cyanide poisonings, Sterling executives believe, have opened a new opportunity for their own acetaminophen drug in this country. Early in 1983, the company launched a $100 million advertising campaign for "world-proven" Panadol.

What will that $100 million be spent on? Marketing surveys and consumer analyses. The planning and preparing of an overall advertising strategy. Ads in newspapers, in magazines, on radio, and most expensive of all, on television. A sixty-second television commercial during a popular evening prime-time program can cost hundreds of thousands of dollars, not counting the expense of making the ad.

Expensive as drug advertising is, it can be worth it. Between 1955 and 1981, Tylenol's advertising won the drug 37 percent of the United States painkiller market. By mid-1982, Tylenol sales represented just over 10 percent of the entire OTC drug market here. Clearly, advertising can produce sales.

What else can it accomplish? What is the effect of OTC drug advertising on the American public?

Drug company executives and their advertising agents answer that the effect is to keep us fully informed about the nonprescription medications available to us. From ads, we learn what drugs we can buy, and where to buy them. We learn how to use them. We can compare various brands—Tylenol and Bayer, Vicks and Coricidin, Dulcolax and Metamucil. We can decide which pill or cream fits our needs best. We can find out how much each drug costs.

Information like this can be helpful. Learning about relative costs, for example, allows consumers to save money. Ads reveal that in 1983, a 100-tablet bottle of Bayer aspirin cost $1.96. A 100-tablet bottle of Bufferin cost $2.91. Regular-strength Tylenol, in the 100-capsule size, was selling for $5.90. For anyone who is not allergic to aspirin, the savings could be substantial.

Savings can be even more substantial with generic OTC drugs. "Generic" means "of the same kind." Most supermarkets and drugstores carry generic versions of common OTC drugs under their own names—Topco, Food Club, Rexall, Safeway, and so on. Generic drugs are virtually the same, chemically, as brand name items. Only the name is different—and the price. A check of drugstore advertising shows that, in 1983, a 100-tablet bottle of one generic brand of aspirin cost just fifty-nine cents.

We can learn more fundamental things from over-the-counter drug advertising as well. We learn that taking care of ourselves is important. We learn that we don't have to put up with aching backs or stuffy noses—we can help ourselves back to health.

We can help others, too. Much OTC drug advertising consists of vignettes of loving family life—scene after scene of wives fetching aspirin and chest rubs for their husbands; mothers caring solicitously for their children; or grown-up children offering laxatives, dental adhesives, and backache remedies to their aging parents and acquaintances. Care for your friends, care for your family, care for yourself—that's one message of over-the-counter drug advertising.

Still, ads don't tell the whole story. Relying on ads alone will not inform consumers of all they need to know about nonprescription medicines.

Every OTC drug ad claims that the product it is promoting is the most effective medication for a particular ailment. Every other similar product is inferior, each ad implies. But few ads give much solid information to back up the claims. Few give consumers the full facts they need to help them decide whether one of several nearly identical preparations is truly the most effective. In short, critics say, drug ads tell us little about the drugs themselves.

Take ads for Tylenol and other acetaminophen pain relievers, such as Datril, Panadol, and Anacin 3. From them, you could find out that some people have an allergic reaction to aspirin, and that these individuals should take a nonaspirin compound. That is an important fact.

However, it is a fact that is of concern to relatively few people. Most of us are not allergic to aspirin. Those who are undoubtedly know about it, and know they should use acetaminophen. So, although acetaminophen advertising gives the public valid information, it is information that not many of us really need.

It would be more to the point if acetaminophen ads included the fact that this substance does little to relieve arthritis pain. Arthritis is a more common complaint than severe aspirin allergy. The fact that acetaminophen is largely ineffective against arthritis, however, is a fact that you are unlikely to come across in advertising for that drug.

Ads for other products similarly lack essential facts. In all the advertising for phenacetin pain relievers, there was no intimation that large amounts of the drug could cause cancer, blood disease, or kidney failure. Yet these were facts that everyone who bought the drug should have been made aware of.

Even when a drug ad does mention facts about a product, it may present them in a confusing way. In television ads for one backache remedy, a voice announces that this drug is the only pain reliever that contains magnesium salicylate. Sounds impressive—but what is magnesium salicylate? A supereffective analgesic, the ad seems to suggest.

Magnesium salicylate is an analgesic, and it is effective. It is a form of salicylic acid—aspirin. So how does this backache pill compare to plain aspirin or acetaminophen? The ad does not say. Nor does it point out that people who are allergic to aspirin probably should not take this remedy either.

Some advertising "facts" are even more questionable. An example is Sterling's charge regarding experts' "concern" about acetaminophen. So far, experts seem thoroughly satisfied with acetaminophen's safety. The Sterling ad did not inform. It confused and misled.

A few ads present "facts" that, according to the FDA, are simply untrue. As 1983 began, there were over eight hundred nonprescription cough medicines on the market. Many were supposed to suppress—stop—a cough. Of all the ingredients advertised as effective suppressants, the FDA found, only three actually did any good at all.

Other cough mixtures are expectorants, which are designed to help a person get rid of the phlegm that can cause a cough. Hundreds of products are advertised as containing effective expectorants. But the FDA found that, by its standards, there is no effective expectorant agent in any OTC cough medicine.

Can anything be done to keep OTC drug manufacturers from making false claims? The answer is yes—sort of.

The responsibility for enforcing truth-in-advertising rules belongs to the Federal Trade Commission (FTC). Over the years, the FTC has taken action against many misleading ads, in print and on the air. Some of these ads have been for nonprescription drugs. For example, the

FTC has warned Sterling Drug about some of its advertising in the past.

However, it is not easy for the FTC to keep false or misleading claims from being seen or heard. Before it can order an ad off the air or out of print, the agency must give the advertiser the opportunity to prove that the claim is accurate. Companies have learned that they can put off producing such proof month after month. While they delay, the ad continues to run. Even if the company eventually admits that it cannot prove its claim, and the ad is removed, millions of people will have seen it.

In the future, the FTC could find enforcement even harder. Early in the 1980s, FTC chairman James Miller III proposed limiting the agency's power to intervene in what he called "marginal cases." According to an article in *Science,* the magazine of the American Association for the Advancement of Science, such cases would be those that involve "extreme exaggeration," that describe an independent, "potentially unproved" analysis, and that "distort the attributes of inexpensive products."

In Miller's view, the change is needed. The FTC has been interfering too much in product advertising, he believes. Asking companies to perform tests to back up their advertising claims put an unfair financial burden on them. "The FTC needs to study whether the costs imposed . . . exceed the benefits derived in the form of reduced fraud and deception," he told a Senate committee.

Many people, including several other FTC commissioners, disagree. One, Patricia Bailey, contended that putting Miller's proposals into effect would "paralyze enforcement." She pointed out that it would mean shifting the burden of proof from manufacturers to consumers. Instead of requiring advertisers to be honest with the public, it would require members of the public to demonstrate that the advertisers were lying or exaggerating. Under Miller's proposals, it would be harder than ever for consumers to judge which OTC drugs are best for them, Bailey and other critics say.

Being able to make that judgment is essential, because although some OTC drugs have little value, others can do much to improve people's health and well-being. And ads—fair, honest ads—can help consumers decide which drugs are which.

Ads can also inform people about useful new products they might not otherwise hear about, members of the American drug industry remind their critics. An example concerns fluoride.

For years, ads have promoted the idea that using a toothpaste containing fluoride will help reduce dental decay. The ads have been convincing, and millions of Americans have switched to fluoride toothpastes. Has it helped? Studies released by the American Dental Society show that this nation's dental health has improved in recent years.

In addition, ads can give specific instructions about how to use nonprescription medicines: two tablets every four hours; one capsule twice a day; apply before bedtime; take as needed. Consumers can learn much about drugs, and about how to use them, from ads. Drug manufacturers and advertisers speak proudly of this fact.

Yet others see a darker, more ominous aspect to advertising that promotes the use of drugs. They worry that the overwhelming message of those ads is that drugs are good for you.

Drugs are good for headaches, backaches, strained muscles, constipation, overtiredness. They're good for getting to sleep, waking up, relaxing, feeling peppier. They're good for dieting, and for settling an upset stomach. Drugs are good for you.

The message has its effect. It brings in $6 billion a year for the American OTC drug industry. Some believe it has another effect as well. They think it has turned this country into a nation of overmedicated men, women, and children.

Many doctors and scientists agree. It is not necessary to take a drug for every ache and pain, they say. If you have a headache, try waiting a few minutes before reaching for the aspirin. The headache may go away. If you're prone to upset stomachs, don't take an antacid. Eat less rich food or smaller portions instead.

Some people claim that drug advertising goes beyond simply making us excessively dependent on OTC medications. They see a link between vast amounts of advertising for legal drugs and the increasing use of illegal drugs in this country.

"Society is giving all of us a double message," according to one expert, Dr. Robert E. Gould. Dr. Gould is a professor of psychiatry at New York Medical College. "On the one hand, we are told, 'Don't take illegal drugs.' At the same time, this is a drug-taking culture and a drug-encouraging culture. Look in anyone's medicine chest and see how many drugs Americans rely on."

Dr. Gould expresses concern about drug advertising. Its overall message, he says, is "that you won't have to suffer, chemistry can give you an answer, the route that drugs offers is the easiest way to get out of anxiety. It focuses on instant gratification, and not on solving the underlying problems."

People who disagree with Dr. Gould scoff at the notion that there could be any connection between taking an aspirin and becoming dependent upon tranquilizers or addicted to heroin. OTC drug advertising is not helping to create a drug problem in this country, they say. Rather, it is essential, because it allows millions of Americans to select and use the nonprescription medications best suited to their needs.

Who is right? OTC drug advertising is all around us. Check it out—and decide for yourself.

...e guidelines, and by February 6, 1984, all OTC
...ffered for sale in the United States, even those
...d from abroad, were supposed to be tamper-
...t. The FDA left it up to each individual company
...lop its own tamper-resistant design, as long as
...ign met federal standards.

...mpliance with the new FDA rules was quick—to
...ith. "Everyone appears to have met the require-
...in time," commented Carol Boyle, executive
... of the Packaging Institute. "The cooperation
...narkable," added another packaging expert.

...emarkable" was the word. In fact, the speed and
...asm with which manufacturers appeared to be
...; the FDA regulation was probably unique in the
...of the American drug industry. Just as Congress
...ponded to the thalidomide and Elixir Sulfanilam-
...edies by passing pure food and drug laws, so OTC
...akers responded to the Tylenol poisonings by
... into tamper-resistant packaging. Without the
...ngs, however, many people thought it unlikely
...: industry would have been so eager. More prob-
...ey say, it would have protested strongly against
...vernment attempt to improve packaging.

...ople had reason to feel that way. The drug indus-
...a history of protesting new FDA rules. Even as it
...esigning OTC packaging, for instance, it was bat-
...e FDA over another proposed guideline. This one
...ed safety warnings on aspirin products.

...e aspirin dispute involved Reye's Syndrome. Sev-
...entific studies have linked this rare disease in chil-
... the taking of aspirin to reduce the fevers that
...any viral illnesses like flu and chicken pox.

...June 1982, the secretary of the Department of
... and Human Services, Richard Schweiker, sent
...) pamphlets warning of the suspected aspirin-
...connection to doctors and pharmacists around

5

DRUG SAFETY

Adam and Stanley Janus died after swallowing cyanide-filled Tylenol capsules on September 29, 1982. Theresa Janus died on September 30, of the same cause. A week later, surviving members of the Janus family were in court, bringing a lawsuit against the company that manufactures Tylenol and the store where the deadly capsules were bought. The suit was in the amount of $25 million.

What were the Januses' chances of proving their case? Their lawyer, Leonard M. Ring, was optimistic. To win, he would have to show that the Tylenol capsules, and the package that contained them, were defective in their design. Ring believed he could do just that.

In filing court papers, Ring pointed out that the bottle of Tylenol in the Janus home had been removed from a shelf in a store. It had been opened and its contents altered. Then it had been replaced. Because the bottle lacked a tamper-resistant cap or lid, and was not sealed with plastic or foil, its eventual purchaser could have had no way of telling that it had been opened before.

Nor could anyone have told that the capsules themselves had been taken apart, emptied, and filled with poison. The capsules, too, could have been sealed, but they were not. This, and the fact that the package itself was unsealed, constituted defects. These defects, Ring contended, made the defendants—Johnson & Johnson and the Jewel food stores—legally liable for the deaths of Adam, Stanley, and Theresa Janus.

Other legal experts were not so sure. They believed the defendants could successfully employ what one professor of law called "the old 'everybody was doing it' defense." Johnson & Johnson was packaging its product in the way most other American drug manufacturers were packaging theirs. Jewel displayed Tylenol bottles on open shelves—just as other stores do. Generally, courts do not find against defendants that are following "common usage" procedures. This is true even if "common usage" does not amount to "the state of the art"—the best known way of doing something.

Leonard Ring was correct about one thing, at least. Both Jewel and Johnson & Johnson could have guarded against product tampering. Nonprescription drugs can be kept behind the counter. Making packages tamper-resistant is possible, as well. It has been the practice in many European countries for years.

Even before the Janus family filed its lawsuit, men and women at Johnson & Johnson and at its subsidiary, McNeil Consumer Products, began designing safer Tylenol packaging. "No one has ever worked so fast," commented one McNeil executive. By early November, the new packages were on the market, and Tylenol was advertising "Safety-sealed new multiple-protection, tamper-resistant packaging."

In going ahead with tamper-resistant packaging, Johnson & Johnson had beaten the FDA to the punch. Not until November, did the agency announce new guidelines of its own. The FDA gave drug companies three months to come up with tamper-resistant designs for drugs in capsule and liquid form. By May 5, 1983, tablets, suppositories, and powders were to be included

This photograph shows
tamper-resistant packag
by the American

5

DRUG SAFETY

Adam and Stanley Janus died after swallowing cyanide-filled Tylenol capsules on September 29, 1982. Theresa Janus died on September 30, of the same cause. A week later, surviving members of the Janus family were in court, bringing a lawsuit against the company that manufactures Tylenol and the store where the deadly capsules were bought. The suit was in the amount of $25 million.

What were the Januses' chances of proving their case? Their lawyer, Leonard M. Ring, was optimistic. To win, he would have to show that the Tylenol capsules, and the package that contained them, were defective in their design. Ring believed he could do just that.

In filing court papers, Ring pointed out that the bottle of Tylenol in the Janus home had been removed from a shelf in a store. It had been opened and its contents altered. Then it had been replaced. Because the bottle lacked a tamper-resistant cap or lid, and was not sealed with plastic or foil, its eventual purchaser could have had no way of telling that it had been opened before.

Nor could anyone have told that the capsules themselves had been taken apart, emptied, and filled with poison. The capsules, too, could have been sealed, but they were not. This, and the fact that the package itself was unsealed, constituted defects. These defects, Ring contended, made the defendants—Johnson & Johnson and the Jewel food stores—legally liable for the deaths of Adam, Stanley, and Theresa Janus.

Other legal experts were not so sure. They believed the defendants could successfully employ what one professor of law called "the old 'everybody was doing it' defense." Johnson & Johnson was packaging its product in the way most other American drug manufacturers were packaging theirs. Jewel displayed Tylenol bottles on open shelves—just as other stores do. Generally, courts do not find against defendants that are following "common usage" procedures. This is true even if "common usage" does not amount to "the state of the art"—the best known way of doing something.

Leonard Ring was correct about one thing, at least. Both Jewel and Johnson & Johnson could have guarded against product tampering. Nonprescription drugs can be kept behind the counter. Making packages tamper-resistant is possible, as well. It has been the practice in many European countries for years.

Even before the Janus family filed its lawsuit, men and women at Johnson & Johnson and at its subsidiary, McNeil Consumer Products, began designing safer Tylenol packaging. "No one has ever worked so fast," commented one McNeil executive. By early November, the new packages were on the market, and Tylenol was advertising "Safety-sealed new multiple-protection, tamper-resistant packaging."

In going ahead with tamper-resistant packaging, Johnson & Johnson had beaten the FDA to the punch. Not until November, did the agency announce new guidelines of its own. The FDA gave drug companies three months to come up with tamper-resistant designs for drugs in capsule and liquid form. By May 5, 1983, tablets, suppositories, and powders were to be included under the guidelines, and by February 6, 1984, all OTC drugs offered for sale in the United States, even those imported from abroad, were supposed to be tamper-resistant. The FDA left it up to each individual company to develop its own tamper-resistant design, as long as that design met federal standards.

Compliance with the new FDA rules was quick—to begin with. "Everyone appears to have met the requirements in time," commented Carol Boyle, executive director of the Packaging Institute. "The cooperation was remarkable," added another packaging expert.

"Remarkable" was the word. In fact, the speed and enthusiasm with which manufacturers appeared to be meeting the FDA regulation was probably unique in the history of the American drug industry. Just as Congress had responded to the thalidomide and Elixir Sulfanilamide tragedies by passing pure food and drug laws, so OTC drug makers responded to the Tylenol poisonings by rushing into tamper-resistant packaging. Without the poisonings, however, many people thought it unlikely that the industry would have been so eager. More probably, they say, it would have protested strongly against any government attempt to improve packaging.

People had reason to feel that way. The drug industry has a history of protesting new FDA rules. Even as it was redesigning OTC packaging, for instance, it was battling the FDA over another proposed guideline. This one concerned safety warnings on aspirin products.

The aspirin dispute involved Reye's Syndrome. Several scientific studies have linked this rare disease in children to the taking of aspirin to reduce the fevers that accompany viral illnesses like flu and chicken pox.

In June 1982, the secretary of the Department of Health and Human Services, Richard Schweiker, sent 150,000 pamphlets warning of the suspected aspirin-Reye's connection to doctors and pharmacists around

This photograph shows several examples of tamper-resistant packaging being developed by the American drug industry.

shame that a trusted drug used by millions of people would be discouraged," he said.

The lawsuit angered Dr. Sidney M. Wolfe, director of the Health Research Group. It was an effort to silence his organization and to "shut the government up," he complained. "The lawsuit shows the committee cares more about the health of the aspirin industry . . . than the health of children," Dr. Wolfe told news reporters.

That was a serious charge. Yet the Committee on the Care of Children was founded to represent aspirin makers, and it was getting its funds from two principal sources, Sterling Drug, makers of Bayer aspirin, and Schering-Plough, makers of St. Joseph aspirin. No doubt executives at both companies are interested in children's health and welfare. But they are also interested in selling aspirin. They believe that, given the small percentage of children who develop Reye's and the uncertainty about exactly why they do develop it, they are justified in opposing a warning plan that could cut into aspirin sales.

Aspirin warnings are not the only matter over which the FDA and the OTC drug industry have been at odds. The industry has taken stands against other proposed warnings—warnings about the use of aspirin by pregnant women, for instance, and about the tendency of some drugs to produce sleepiness or dizziness.

The industry also protested a requirement that medicine containers be made "child-proof." Consumer groups argued that child guard caps could save hundreds of children from accidental poisonings each year. Drug manufacturers responded that such caps can be difficult to work, even for adults. They would be a major inconvenience to many people, particularly to the elderly and the handicapped.

Did the drug industry protest against child guard caps because of concern for old or crippled people? Or was it worried that people might not use so many aspirins and sleeping pills and laxatives if they had to struggle to open the containers?

The industry has put up a strong battle to continue selling products that the FDA considers unsafe or ineffective—or both. Years ago, scientific studies showed conclusively that large amounts of phenacetin, taken over a long period of time, could produce serious, sometimes fatal, side effects. Yet, the producers of phenacetin products, stressing the words "large" and "long," argued that they should be permitted to go on selling the drug. Finally, in 1982, the FDA ordered it off the market. Until July 1983, the public remained at risk from phenacetin.

Perhaps that wasn't so bad in the case of phenacetin, which seems to cause damage only with excessive amounts. But some drugs really could be dangerous, capable of doing a great deal of damage in a short time and at the recommended dosage. The so-called booze blockers are an example, most experts say.

What can the FDA do to protect us against such drugs? There are two possibilities: seizure and recall. Under federal law, the FDA can seize any drug (or food, device, or cosmetic) that is adulterated or mislabeled. For example, suppose that during the manufacturing process, lead accidently gets into a batch of cough syrup. Lead poisoning can be deadly. The adulteration comes to the FDA's attention. The agency applies for a court order authorizing seizure of the entire shipment of contaminated syrup.

Seizure can be a useful tool, but it is also an awkward one, because the FDA can only seize one shipment at a time. If three or four separate shipments of the cough syrup mixture show lead contamination, the FDA will have to obtain three or four separate court orders. This can be expensive and time-consuming and it is why the agency frequently relies on recall of dangerous or harmful products.

Recall is a voluntary procedure. The FDA cannot force a company to announce one. It was Johnson & Johnson, and not the FDA, that made the decision to recall Tylenol products in 1982.

In undertaking the recall, Johnson & Johnson acted promptly and responsibly. Not all companies are so public-spirited. In the case of companies that are not, the FDA is compelled to use publicity.

Let's go back to our imaginary lead-in-cough-syrup example. Suppose the adulteration is widespread, so widespread that the FDA cannot hope to use seizure to keep all bottles of the mixture out of the hands of the public. Yet the company that makes the medicine refuses to order a recall.

So the FDA calls in the news media. Press releases are prepared. Stories go out to newspapers and magazines, to radio and TV stations. Before long, millions of people know about the contamination. They also know that the drug company is unwilling to protect the public.

This is not the sort of publicity the company wants. If it continues, people may never buy its products again. Eventually, company executives give in and announce a recall. Thus, the FDA's ability to get a recall is considerable, even though it lacks the force of law.

Drug companies slow to recall defective products, eager to fight proposed safety rules, opposed to the FDA on issue after issue—this doesn't sound much like the kind of glad cooperation that went into the tamper-resistant packaging effort during the fall of 1982. What made that case different?

In the first place, there was the massive publicity. Virtually every person alive in the United States knew about the Tylenol tampering. They knew that other products, too, were being tampered with. Their buying habits changed, and OTC drug sales dropped sharply. The industry realized it would have to go into safer packaging—or see sales continue to drop. It had a "clear profit motivation" to move into tamper-resistant packaging, according to James D. Cope, president of the Proprietary Association, a trade group.

In the second place, it was clear that, at least for a time, there would be a public outcry for laws to require tamper-resistant packaging. It would only be a question of what kind of tamper-resistant packaging. And that, for the industry, was the problem.

On October 4, 1982, Cook County, Illinois—the county in which the first Tylenol deaths occurred—passed a law requiring all over-the-counter medications to be "enclosed in sealed containers." No other form of tamper-resistant packaging, no matter how effective, would be legal there.

The state of California passed a new drug packaging law, too, but it was different from the Cook County statute. Around the country, other state legislatures and city councils were also considering passing tamper-resistant laws.

There was no way, drug company executives knew, that they could keep up with such a hodgepodge of state and local laws. OTC drugs are made to be sold nationwide. It would not be economically possible for a company to produce a drug and package it in various ways in order to meet fifty or more different packaging codes. The only solution was regulations that would apply to nonprescription drugs sold throughout the country.

By October 5, the Proprietary Association had a proposal ready for the FDA. It recommended that the agency issue general rules on tamper-resistant packaging and leave decisions about specific designs to the individual companies. The group outlined eleven possible forms of packaging that would be acceptable to the industry, while still protecting the public. The FDA guidelines, announced just over a month later, generally reflected the association's recommendations.

That, however, is not the end of the story. In September 1983, five months before the FDA's final packaging guidelines were due to take effect, the agency announced it was extending its deadline. No longer would drug companies be required to package all products in tamper-resistant containers by February of the next year. In fact, there would be no deadline for the companies at all.

Why not? The FDA cited pressure from the drug industry as the reason for abandoning its new rule.

In the days that followed, the FDA action received little attention in the news media. People's confidence in OTC drugs, and in their safety, seemed to have been restored. Already, Tylenol had regained 30 percent of the nonprescription pain-killer market, just 7 percent less than it had had before the cyanide deaths. What's more, people in the industry noted, the majority of OTC drug manufacturers had begun using sealed containers. The indefinite extension of the tamper-resistant rule would not alter that fact, they said.

Consumer activists were unconvinced. Without specific government standards, they argued, drug companies might well decide to discontinue tamper-resistant packaging in the months and years ahead.

By October 1983, however, Americans had new protection against over-the-counter drug tampering. In that month President Ronald Reagan signed the Federal Antitampering Act into law. It provides for a $10,000 fine and a ten-year jail sentence for anyone convicted of attempting to tamper. If tampering results in a death, the convicted tamperer may be fined up to $100,000. He or she could be imprisoned for life.

So by the end of 1983, drug tampering no longer seemed to be the threat it had been a year earlier. Now, though, the public faces a new threat from OTC drugs. Or so some Americans believe. That threat—if it is one—comes directly from the FDA.

6

DRUG "SWITCHING" AND DEREGULATION

What is an over-the-counter drug?

An over-the-counter drug is relatively mild and non-addictive. Its effects are generally known. For thirty years, an OTC drug has been one that most experts have agreed could be used by millions of people without a doctor's prescription. Now, that may be changing. Within a few years, hundreds of new, potent, and potentially habit-forming medicines may be available over the counter to the American public.

The reason for the change goes back to 1962 and to the amendments to the 1938 Food, Drug, and Cosmetics Act that Congress passed that year. Those amendments required the FDA to make sure that all the drugs sold in the United States are safe and effective. Consequently, the FDA undertook two separate studies, the Drug Efficacy Study Investigation Review (DESI Review), for prescription medicines, and the Over-the Counter Review (OTC Review), for nonprescription items.

The DESI Review began in 1962, and involved the investigation of about five thousand drugs. The OTC Review got under way ten years later. At the outset, it appeared to be an enormous project, involving the study of three hundred thousand or more different OTC drugs.

The FDA, however, reduced the study to manageable size by deciding to investigate only the one thousand active ingredients in those three hundred thousand drugs. The ingredients were divided into twenty-seven classes, and assigned to seventeen different panels of experts. The experts included pharmacists, toxicologists, doctors, dentists, and representatives from the drug industry and from consumer groups.

The DESI and OTC reviews involved more than simply ordering drug tests. The agency's panels were also charged with considering whether or not drugs were properly classed as prescription or nonprescription. Behind this requirement lay the conviction of members of Congress—and of most people in the drug industry— that many prescription-only drugs actually ought to be available over the counter. Thus, an important part of the FDA's mandate was to consider moving large numbers of drugs from prescription to nonprescription status.

The FDA did consider such moves, and by the early 1980s, the switching process had begun. By now, the results are apparent. More and more former prescription items are appearing on open shelves and counters. An example is Actifed, a popular cold decongestant. Eventually, even powerful antibiotics like penicillin may be switched.

The drug switch will do much to improve the health of Americans, its advocates claim. Being able to buy sophisticated medications over the counter will save patients money, for instance. Not having to go to a doctor every time they need a prescription will allow them to keep their medical bills down. In addition, since OTC drugs generally cost less than prescription medicines, people will save at the drugstore, too. Saving money will make people more willing—and more able—to seek out medical care when they need it.

The drug switch will also save time and trouble, say its proponents. People won't have to take a day off to go to the doctor whenever they have a cold and need Actifed, for example. They won't have to make appointment after appointment to renew prescriptions for medication to control high blood pressure, asthma, or other chronic conditions.

That saving of time can be important for anyone, the drug switch advocates point out, but it could be of special benefit to families in rural America. In some places, people have to travel for an hour or more to reach a doctor. Others who might find it particularly helpful include those who live in run-down or slum areas of large cities. Few private doctors practice in such neighborhoods, and clinics and hospitals there are frequently rushed and overcrowded. In city slum and remote countryside alike, emergencies may arise in which people cannot get to a doctor. Yet, as the prescription-to-nonprescription switches continue, it should become easier for even these people to obtain the medicines they need.

However, saving time and money, important as they may prove to be, are not the only reasons for enthusiasm about FDA drug switching. To many people, the main attraction of the program is that it will allow patients to take more responsibility for their own health. Self-care and self-medication, they believe, represent the wave of the future.

Americans today take a tremendous interest in health and physical fitness. In cities, drivers and pedestrians are hard put to dodge joggers of all ages and sizes. Joggers appear in the suburbs and on country roads, too, along with bicyclers and walkers. People are signing up for exercise classes. They are swimming, learning aerobic dancing, playing tennis, buying exercise bicycles and

*As many prescription drugs become
available over-the-counter, will health-
conscious Americans confidently be able
to prescribe medicines for themselves?*

rowing machines, and much more. In the 1980s Americans are trying as never before to improve their health through programs of vigorous exercise.

And through diet. For years, Americans have dieted and changed their eating habits in an effort to look thin and fashionable. Now, millions are using diet, not just to look better, but to feel better as well.

That means more than just giving up desserts, or changing from regular soda to a low-calorie diet brand. It means eating more vegetables, which provide needed vitamins and minerals, and less red meat, which, doctors say, can contribute to heart disease and to some cancers. It means cutting down on salt, which has been linked to high blood pressure. It means substituting dark flours, rye and whole wheat, for refined white flour; limiting the use of refined white sugar; and eating more whole grains.

Making such wholesale changes in diet requires real effort. The fact that so many Americans are making that effort suggests that they will be willing to make the effort to prescribe medicines for themselves, proponents of the drug switch say.

Not only that, they will also be capable of making that effort carefully and wisely. Americans are exceptionally well informed about health care, switch supporters maintain.

Much of their information comes through newspaper and magazine articles. Many newspapers print regular health-care columns, as well as news stories about up-to-date medical findings. Magazine articles deal with similar subjects. Popular periodicals devoted entirely to health and nutrition include *Prevention, Health,* and *Weight Watchers Magazine.*

People are also turning to books in their search for better health. In the spring of 1982, the *New York Times* paperback best-seller list included one diet book and two exercise books. Its hardcover list showed two exercise books and three on diet.

Still another source of health information is advertising. Thanks to print ads and to broadcast commercials for thousands of OTC drug products, Americans know a great deal about what medicines are available to them, how those medicines work, and how they ought to be used. So far, that information does not extend to prescription items, because the FDA does not allow direct consumer advertising of prescription drugs. But as the prescription-to-nonprescription switches continue, drug companies will change their advertising to match. Gradually, we will become better and better informed about medicines that, until now, few of us have ever heard of.

People are knowledgeable enough today to care for their own health, drug switch advocates say, and they are willing to care for it. Therefore, they ought to be given every opportunity to do so. After all, many doctors are convinced that even the best medicine is only as good as the patient. Unless a person is actively involved in his or her health care, that care cannot accomplish all that it should. Getting Americans to take greater responsibility for their health through making more drugs available over the counter, switch supporters say, will mean a healthier America.

Or will it? Some people are convinced that drug switching will lead to a health-care disaster in this country.

In the first place, these people argue, Americans are not really as well informed about health and medicine as they appear to be. Sure, Americans see and hear a lot about medical matters. But what they are seeing and hearing is not necessarily reliable.

Nearly all drug advertising is self-serving. It has one purpose above all—to sell a product. Although it loudly proclaims the virtues of this or that preparation, it rarely says anything about any drawbacks the product may have—its possible side effects, or the cases in which it should not be used. Ads for formerly prescription-only items are not likely to be any more complete.

Of course, people can turn to newspapers, books, and magazines for information. The magazine *Consumer Reports,* for example, carries investigative articles about various OTC medications. *The 1976 Handbook of Prescription Drugs,* by Drs. Richard Burack and Fred J. Fox, and *Pills That Don't Work,* by the Health Research Group, are two sources of information about the benefits and drawbacks of prescription drugs. Many of these drugs are, or soon will be, available over the counter. A good source of information on nonprescription drugs is *Over the Counter Pills That Don't Work,* by the Health Research Group.

Whether or not people will refer to such books is another matter. Doctors do not seem to have used them. Many of the drugs listed in each book as being of little or no medical value are among the most frequently prescribed medications in the country. If doctors are not always adequately informed about the drugs they recommend, it seems unrealistic to expect the general public to do any better.

Carefully researched books such as these by Burack and Fox and the Health Research Group can be a good source of information about health matters, but books on a best-seller list may be less certain. Some present well-rounded programs of diet and exercise, but many others do not. Some promote fad programs that seem to have been designed solely to earn a profit for their inventors. A few suggest regimens that most doctors condemn as dangerous. Americans who rely on such popular sources may not really know very much about good health practices after all, experts warn.

Are Americans really prepared to take over their own health care? In 1967, the president of the American

Pharmaceutical Association, William Apple, remarked that "self-medication is being practiced today with a degree of sophistication that belongs in the Dark Ages." Some people fear that little has changed in the fifteen years since. Speaking in 1982 at a symposium sponsored by the Proprietary Association, which favors drug switching, Matt Clark, the medical editor of *Newsweek* magazine, said, "Sometimes I'm not too confident that large numbers of people are really ready to take important medical matters into their own hands, at least judging from some of the letters I get from readers."

Critics of drug switching also worry about what may happen when Americans begin using potent drugs without medical supervision. In the case of one asthma remedy, reaction was swift. In October 1982, the FDA approved switching metaproterenol sulfate from prescription to nonprescription status. This drug, inhaled by asthma victims, is very effective in relieving their wheezing and shortness of breath. Yet when the switch was announced, many leading doctors condemned it.

Used according to a doctor's instructions, they said, metaproterenol sulfate is safe. But if people were to just pick the drug up off the shelf and use it without those instructions, they might be in trouble. Overuse of the inhaler might cause cardiac arrest or respiratory failure. "Patients might wind up in the hospital more frequently, they'll be sicker when they get there, and there is a possibility that we might face an epidemic of deaths among asthmatics," protested Dr. Leslie Hendeles, asssociate professor of pharmacy at the University of Florida.

Advocates of the switch answered that such worries were groundless. They pointed out that at least one potent drug, insulin, has been available over the counter for years. Insulin must be used regularly by people with diabetes, in order to control the amount of sugar in their blood. Going without it can mean illness, coma, and death. That's why insulin has been classed as nonprescription—so that those who need it can always get it in an emergency simply by walking into a drugstore and asking for it. Diabetics have demonstrated that they are perfectly capable of using the drug wisely, switch proponents point out. Asthma sufferers and people with other chronic illnesses can do the same.

Nevertheless, the FDA responded to the critics of the metaproteronol sulfate switch. In May 1983, the agency reached an agreement with the drug's manufacturers to return it to prescription-only status.

Critics of switching are doubtful about making other potent drugs available over the counter. Health conditions can change, they say. Over time, a person's high blood pressure might get better—or worse. Either change could require a change in medication. But if high blood pressure medicine were available without prescription, patients might go for years and years without seeing a doctor. Changes in their condition would go undetected, and that could be fatal. The same is true of people with other health problems.

Another difficulty people might face if they try to dose themselves without medical supervision is a dangerous mixing of drugs. Careful doctors always check with patients about the medicines they are taking before prescribing anything new. They know that certain drugs should not be taken together. In some cases, two drugs may cancel each other out, so the patient benefits from neither. In other cases, the combination may produce serious illness. Pharmacists, too, may keep track of their customers' prescriptions in order to make sure harmful drug combinations do not occur. But as more drugs are switched to OTC status, no professional will be able to warn people if they mix drugs improperly.

Allergies could be another problem. Many people, for instance, are seriously allergic to penicillin and to other antibiotics. Yet there are those who argue in favor of making penicillin available over the counter. If that happens, people who develop an allergic reaction might fail to recognize that condition for what it is. They might just believe the reaction is a symptom of disease—and go right on taking the medication.

Finally, critics wonder how much money drug switching will save in the long run. Self-medication can have hidden costs. According to the National Arthritis Foundation, Americans waste $1 billion a year on phony "cures" for that disease.

Critics of drug switching concede that people will save money on doctor and hospital visits if the program continues. But that saving may mean ignoring certain health problems, problems that will grow more serious as time goes by. Eventually, those problems will have to be treated—and the bills paid. People may end up taking expensive medicines or having operations that could have been avoided if they had had professional medical care earlier.

Arguments between those who favor drug switching and those who oppose it are sure to continue. Switching is likely to continue, too. Classifying more and more drugs as nonprescription, and giving people the opportunity for increased self-medication, are just part of a general trend toward less government regulation in the U.S.

The deregulation trend, which began emerging in the 1970s, has affected several agencies of the federal government. The proposal of FTC chairman James Miller to limit that agency's control over misleading advertising is part of that trend. So was the FDA decision not to require tamper-resistant packaging after all.

In fact, many people in and out of government feel that FDA deregulation ought to go beyond the relabeling of prescription and nonprescription medicines. They argue that the FDA has gained too much control over the entire drug industry. That control severely limits the industry's ability to develop and market valuable new drugs, they say.

Getting a drug from test tube to store shelf is an expensive process. It is made more expensive by overregulation, industry leaders charge. Between 1963 and 1976, it cost about $50 million to put a new drug on the market. Today, it costs $70 million.

Part of that increase can be explained by inflation. Prices for almost everything have risen tremendously over the last few years. But the extra cost is also due in part to FDA rules, which have required more and more careful testing for safety and effectiveness over the years.

That extra cost may force a drug manufacturer to give up testing a compound even before scientists can be sure whether or not that compound is a useful one. If the first test results are poor, company executives may decide to put the compound aside and concentrate instead on improving or altering a drug that has already been shown to work. No one knows how many lifesaving drugs may be sitting, their testing discontinued, in America's pharmaceutical laboratories.

Overregulation occurs at later stages, as well, many people believe. The FDA will not accept tests and studies unless they are carried out in strict accordance with agency standards. That is neither fair nor necessary, industry representatives say. They agree that the FDA has a responsibility to make sure American drug products are safe and effective, but if a study shows that a drug is both, they say, the FDA should accept that study, even if it was not done precisely according to a certain set of rules.

Cost isn't the only problem that may have been created by FDA rules. Time is a difficulty, too.

It takes years for a new drug to win FDA approval. During that time, hundreds of people may die from the very disease the drug was meant to cure. Those lives might have been saved if FDA regulations were less rigid.

Time is a problem in another way. A drug manufacturer takes out a patent as soon as a drug is discovered, and that patent lasts for seventeen years. Yet by the time the drug is approved for sale, seven or eight years may have gone by. During half the time the drug is protected by the patent, the drug company is unable to make any money on it.

Such problems make the development of new drugs look unattractive to manufacturers. FDA rules about drug safety and warning labels hamper marketing and sales. Only if the FDA deregulates—requires less testing and less rigorous testing, and fewer warnings and safety devices—will the American drug industry be able to continue offering important new drugs to the public.

That's one side of the argument—the deregulators' side. Other people defend the FDA requirements. They contend that the drug industry has given ample evidence of needing such regulation. It has fought testing requirements, warning labels, and safety devices. It has promoted drugs that it had every reason to suspect of being unsafe. After the Tylenol poisonings, it rushed into tamper-resistant packaging—then backed off.

Those who favor regulation also see merit in slow FDA approval of new drugs. Any American born in the late 1950s or early 1960s can be thankful that Dr. Frances O. Kelsey held up agency approval of thalidomide. More recently, the FDA delayed approving Oraflex, the arthritis medication. Approval finally came and fifty men and women quickly died. That can be taken as evidence that the FDA might have done well to have been even tougher in that case.

Some Americans would like to see the FDA being tougher all around. Far from being too strict, they say, the agency is too lax. It allows people in the drug industry to have too much say in how their business is regulated.

As those who favor stricter regulation see it, a large part of the problem stems from a "revolving door." Some of the people who work for the FDA have come to the agency from the drug industry. Often, when they leave government service, they turn around and go right back into the industry.

In one way, that is reasonable. Men and women from the industry are knowledgeable about it. They are particularly well prepared to consider industry problems and to make decisions about them.

Yet the revolving door has its drawbacks. Sometimes people who have been part of an industry in the past, and who expect to return to it in the future, find it difficult to be objective about regulating that industry. On occasion, such people may be too sympathetic to the industry's point of view. They may find themselves interpreting agency rules in ways that make things easier and more profitable for their friends and colleagues in the industry.

Recently, the revolving door has helped speed the pace of deregulation. Industry leaders—not just in drugs, but in most other industries as well—have been calling for such deregulation. When some of these people are appointed to government agencies, they put their deregulatory ideas into effect. When they return to industry, their places are taken by men and women who have experienced the benefits to industry of that deregulation, and who want to see even more of it.

Will deregulation continue throughout the 1980s? Will increasing numbers of drugs be made available over the counter? Will agencies like the FDA and FTC lose the power they have to oversee the manufacturing, advertising, and selling of nonprescription medications?

Or will the pendulum begin to swing back—back toward regulation?

7

THE ULTIMATE REGULATOR

As the 1980s began, Americans seemed to be rushing toward deregulation. Within three years, however, there were hints that the rush might be slowing down.

One hint came when the drug industry asked the FDA to set national guidelines for tamper-resistant packaging. Even though industry leaders later persuaded the agency to extend its deadline for compliance, the fact remained that those leaders wanted *national* packaging standards. Faced with the prospect of having to meet an unknown number of different packaging rules around the country, manufacturers turned to federal regulators.

Such about-faces could happen again. As federal rules are eased, states, counties, towns, and cities may start coming up with new regulations of their own. That will mean headaches for industry. "If you're a major manufacturer and distributor of products in interstate commerce," says Jeffrey H. Joseph, a vice-president of the Chamber of Commerce, "and have to be worried about conflicting regulations not only of the fifty states but also local jurisdictions, you have a nightmare." If that nightmare becomes reality for the over-the-counter drug industry, this country will almost certainly see a return to stricter federal government regulation.

However, that nightmare may never come to pass for OTC drugs. Basically, Americans trust the nonprescription products they use. Even if federal regulations are made less strict, local governments may not feel public pressure to impose new rules of their own.

It is important to remember that the furor over the need for tamper-resistant packaging arose only because of the Tylenol poisonings. Those poisonings were an out-of-the-ordinary event—one that we hope will not happen again.

Why did it happen in the first place? No one knows. One person, Dr. Daniel Blazer, a professor of psychiatry at the Duke University School of Medicine in North Carolina, has speculated that the poisoner may have wanted to warn consumers about OTC drugs in general. "He may feel he is doing us a favor . . . thinking a few people can get hurt so that more people will be helped," Dr. Blazer suggested at the time of the tragedy.

Most people rejected Dr. Blazer's hypothesis about a well-intentioned murderer. The poisoner acted out some warped, self-serving motivation of his or her own, they thought. But whatever the reason behind the poisonings, they did act as a warning about nonprescription drugs.

The warning was timely. There is little doubt that millions of Americans abuse OTC drugs.

Over-the-counter medications can be very useful. It's hard to imagine life without aspirin, acetaminophen, Mercurochrome, and dozens of other familiar remedies. Used properly, OTC medicines offer quick, relatively inexpensive relief for many common ailments.

Unfortunately, though, Americans tend to be careless about nonprescription drugs. People are not sufficiently critical of advertising. They neglect to compare products and prices. They fail to read directions or pay attention to warning labels. They combine various medications in ways that may be harmful. Above all, Americans overuse the OTC drugs available to them.

The American public needs to learn to be more cautious about OTC drugs. It needs to learn to treat all medicines, prescription as well as nonprescription, with more respect. That will be true no matter what happens in the industry—further deregulation or a swing back to stricter rules and guidelines.

If deregulation increases, Americans will find themselves increasingly on their own in the legal drug market. As drug switching continues, potent and possibly habit-forming drugs will be offered to them directly. Because prescriptions will not be required in many cases, doctors and pharmacists will no longer be in a position to advise patients how to use many drugs wisely.

But even if deregulation does not continue, Americans ought to take on more responsibility with regard to OTC drugs. All the government regulation in the world cannot protect people unless they are willing to protect themselves. In the end, the most important regulator is the individual.

FOR FURTHER READING

Arnow, L. Earle. *Health in a Bottle: Searching for the Drugs That Help.* Philadelphia: J.B. Lippincott Co., 1970.

Burack, Richard, M.D. and Fred J. Fox, M.D. *The 1976 Handbook of Prescription Drugs.* New York: Pantheon, 1976.

Fuller, John G. *200,000,000 Guinea Pigs.* New York: Putnam, 1972.

Handbook of Nonprescription Drugs. Washington, D.C.: American Pharmaceutical Association. 7th ed. 1982.

Health Research Group. *Over the Counter Pills That Don't Work.* New York: Pantheon Press, 1983.

The Proprietary Association. "New Resources in Self-Medication . . . A Symposium, Condensations of Papers and Discussions." Washington, D.C., November 1, 1982.

Weiss, Malcolm E. *Gods, Stars, and Computers.* New York: Doubleday, 1980.

Wolfe, Sidney, M., M.D., Christopher M. Coley, and the Health Research Group. *Pills That Don't Work.* New York: Farrar, Straus & Giroux, 1981.

Zimmerman, David R. *The Essential Guide To Nonprescription Drugs.* New York: Harper & Row. 1983.

INDEX

Shanidar Cave, Iraq, 9
Sober Aid, 25, 30
Sober Up!, 25, 30
Sober Up Time, 25, 30
Sterling Drug, 37, 39, 42–43, 53
Strychnine, 7

Tamper-resistant packaging, 7, 47–48, 49, 50, 55–57, 70, 73–74
Thalidomide, 17–18, 50, 70
Turlington, Robert, 12
200,000,000 Guinea Pigs, 33
Tylenol
  advertising of, 33, 37, 39–41
  development of, 35–37
  poisoning case, 1–2, 3, 5–7, 39, 47, 55–56, 70, 74

safer packaging of, 48, 57
switch from prescription to nonprescription, 17

United States government, 5, 31, 51, 68. *See also* Congress: Department of Agriculture; etc.
Unpatented medicines, 12
Upjohn Company, 31

Warner-Lambert, 31
Weight Watchers Magazine, 63
William S. Merrell Company, 17–18

Zagros Mountain, Iraq, 9
Zomax, 28, 29, 30

ABOUT
THE AUTHOR

Ann E. Weiss was born in Newton, Massachusetts, and was educated at Brown University. She is well known as an author of nonfiction books for young people, several of which have won awards and were recognized as Outstanding Trade Books by the National Council for the Social Studies and the National Science Teachers Association. She is the author of *Polls and Surveys: A Look at Public Opinion Research* for Franklin Watts. Ms. Weiss lives with her husband, Malcolm E. Weiss, and their two daughters in North Whitefield, Maine.